Welcome
to
Botanical Design Adult Coloring Book III

Please visit our website at
www.botanicalartdesigns.com
for more information on
new designs and books.

ISBN: 1515301060
ISBN-13: 978-1515301066

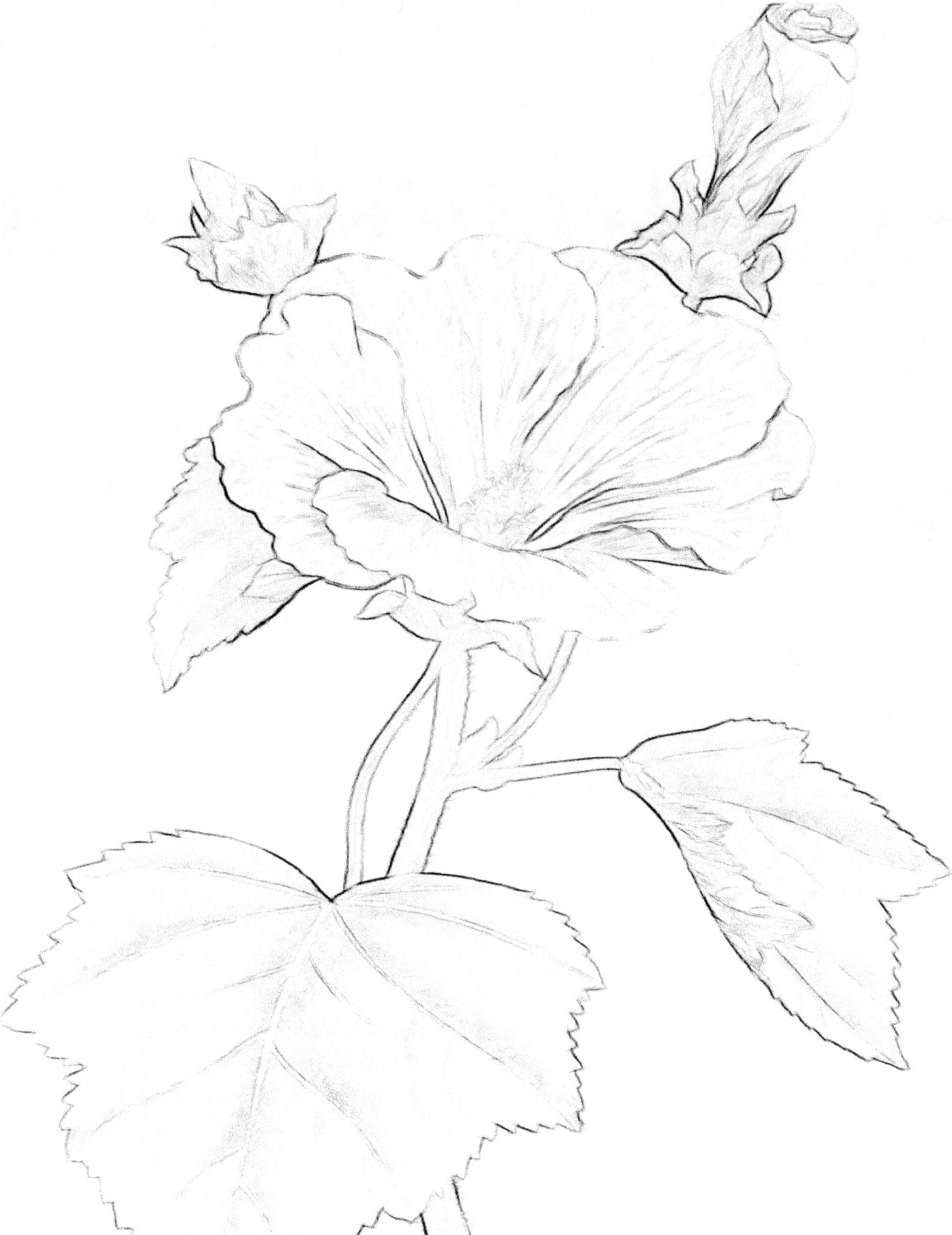

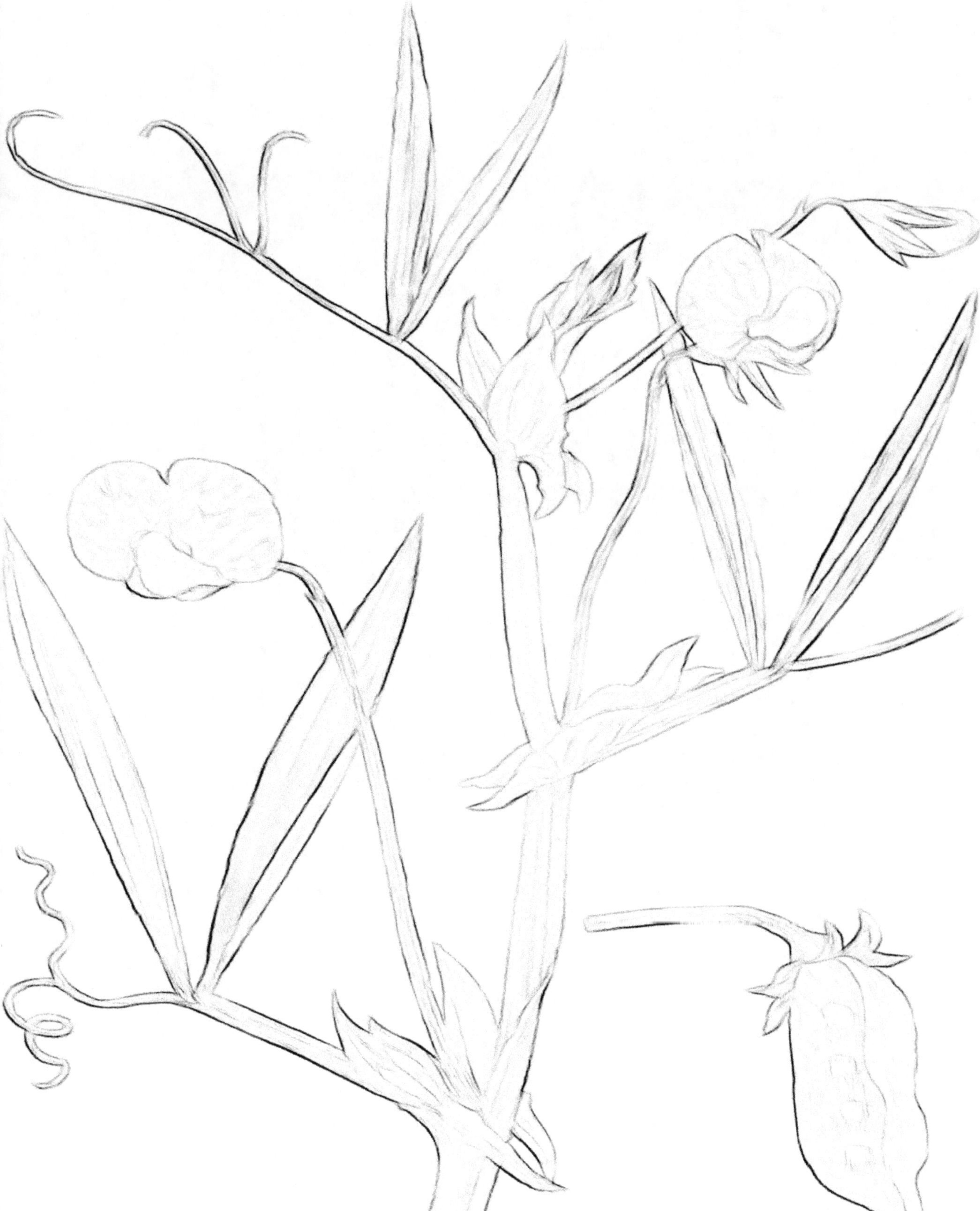

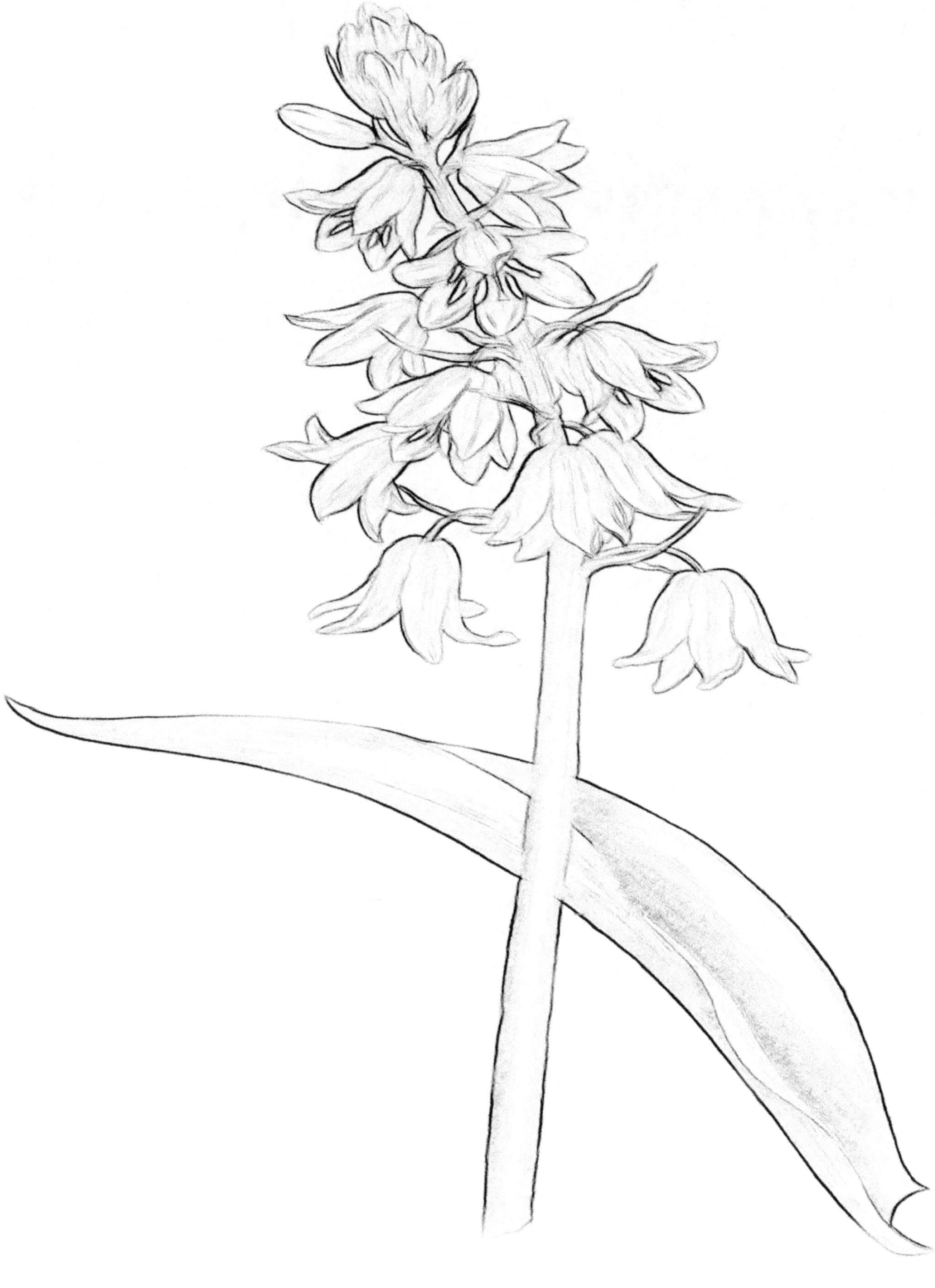

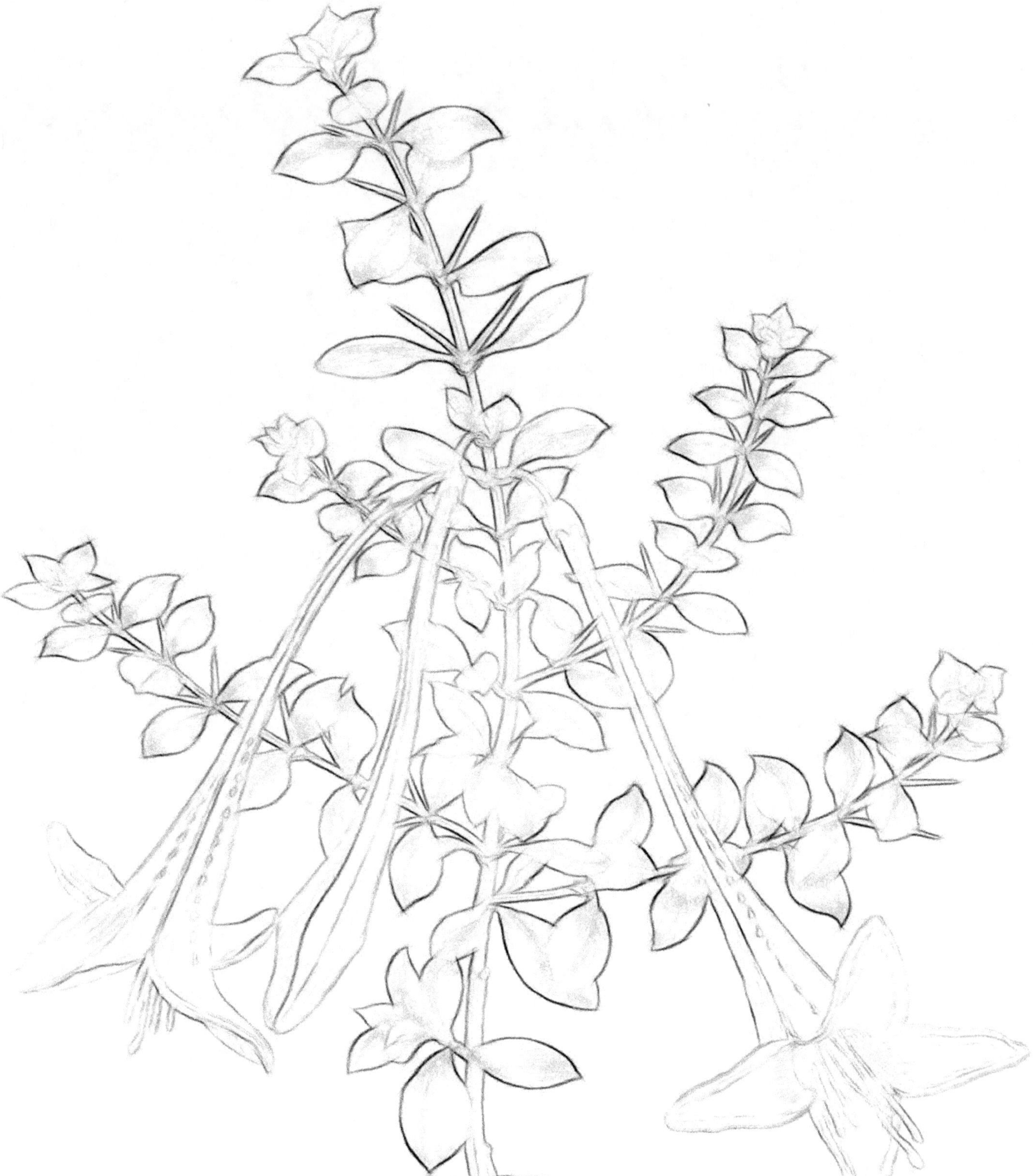

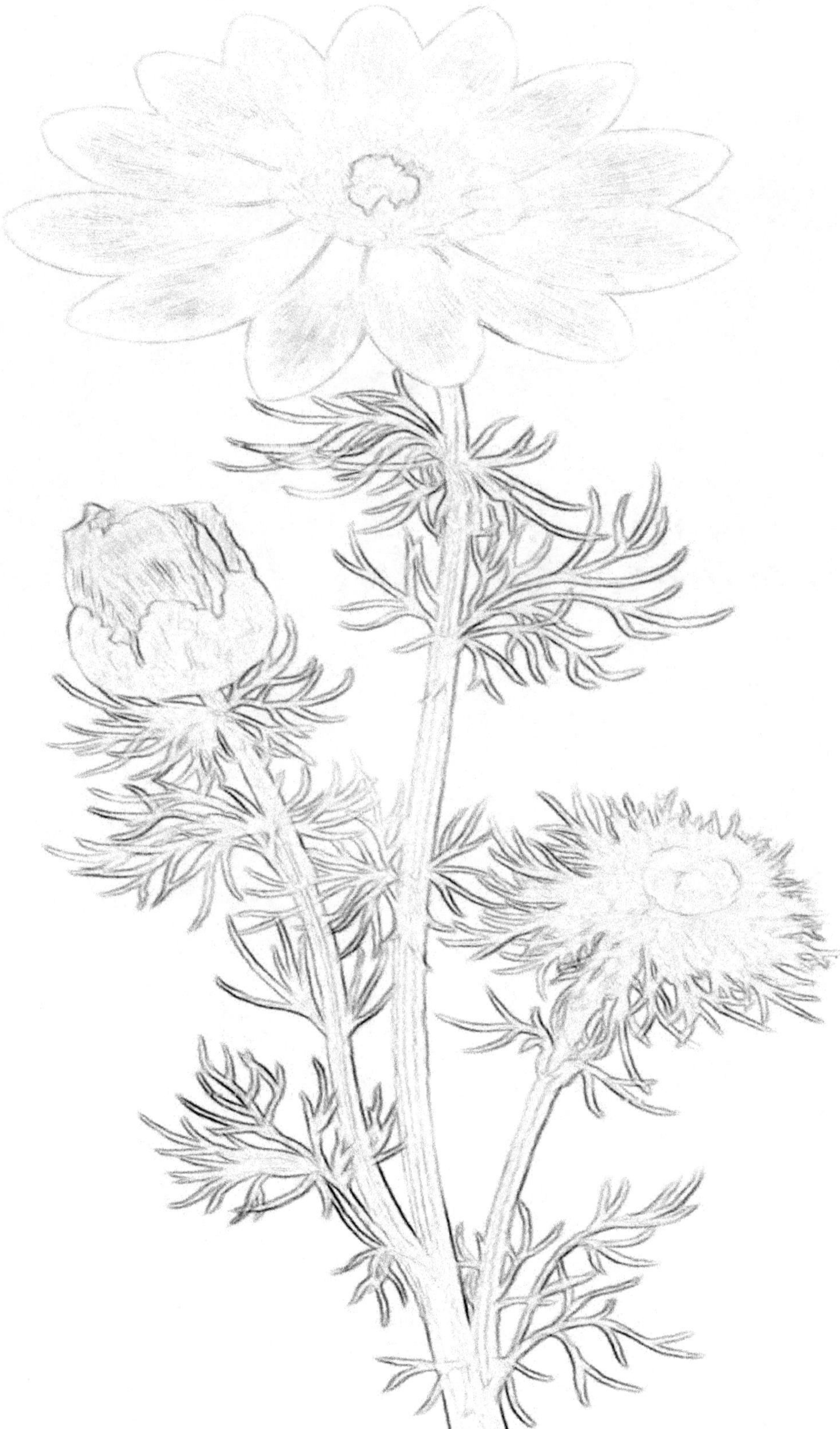

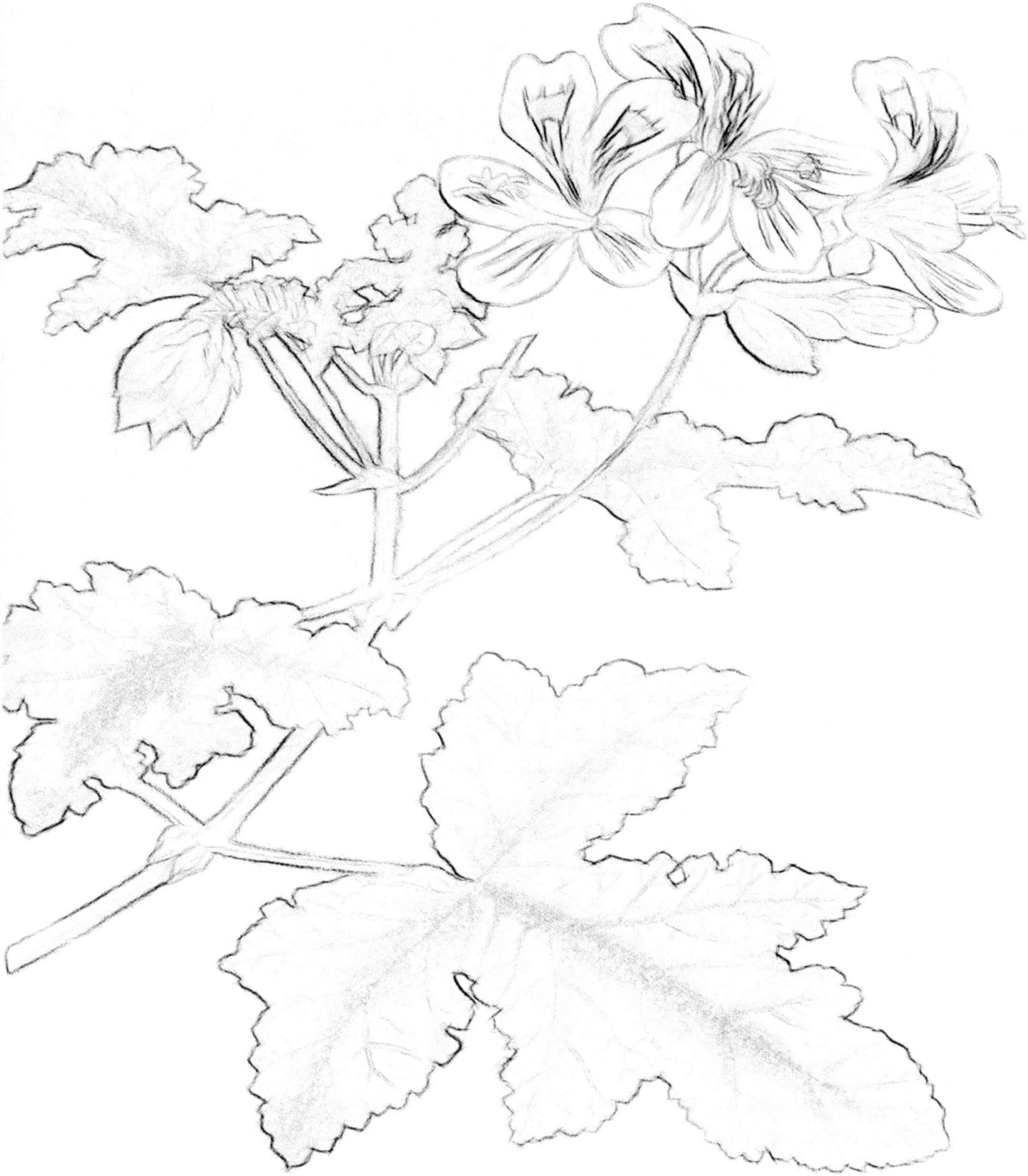

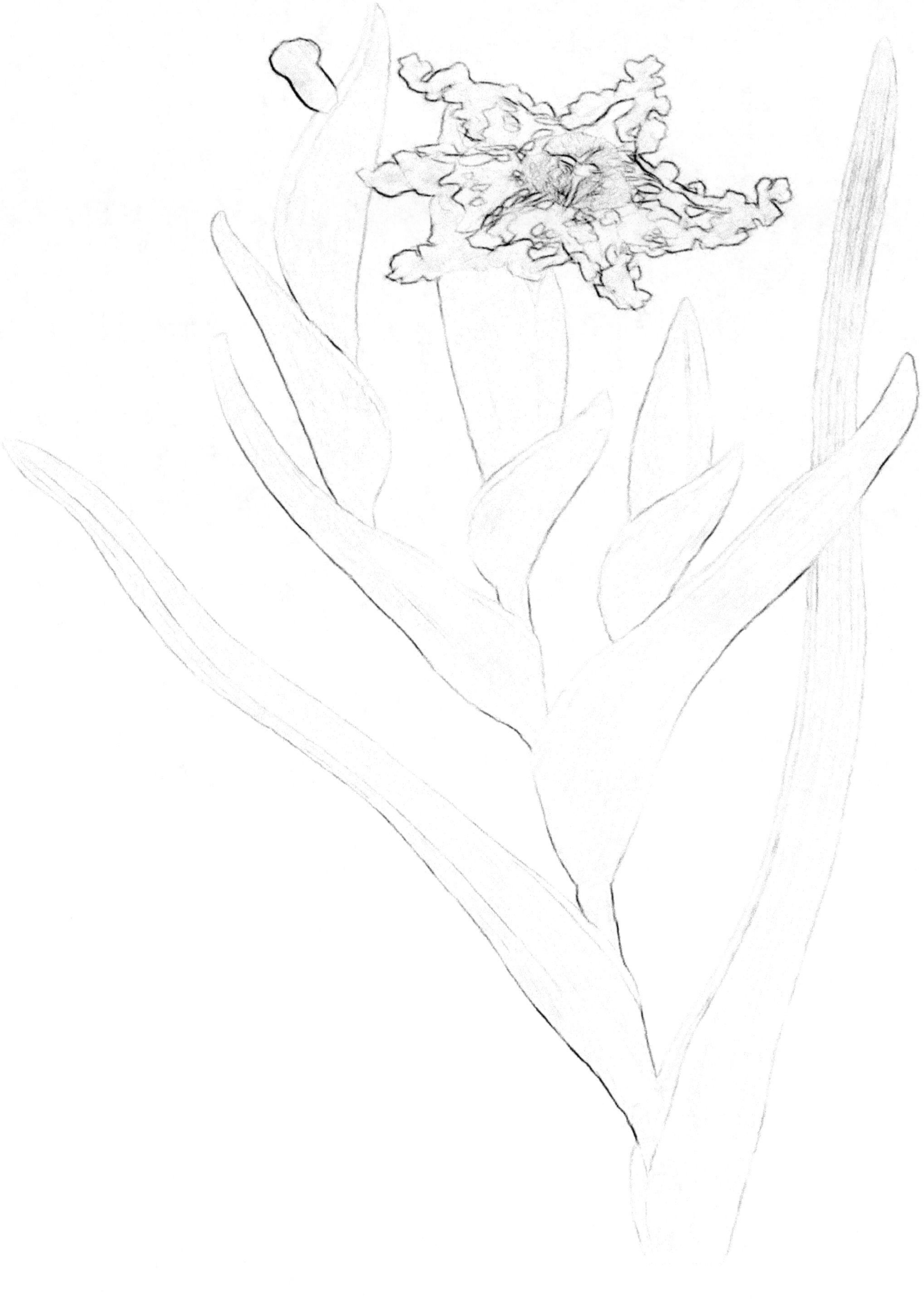

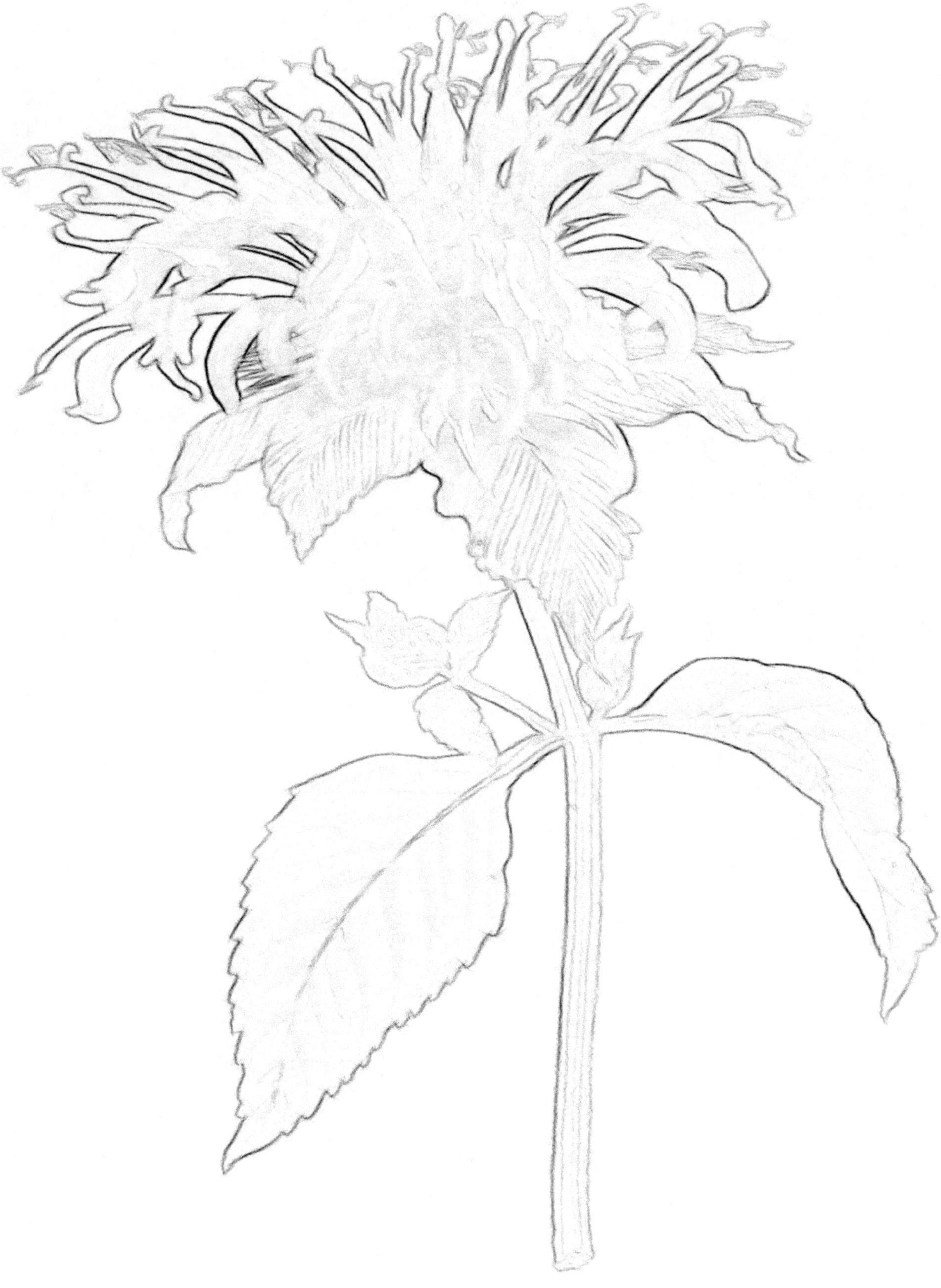

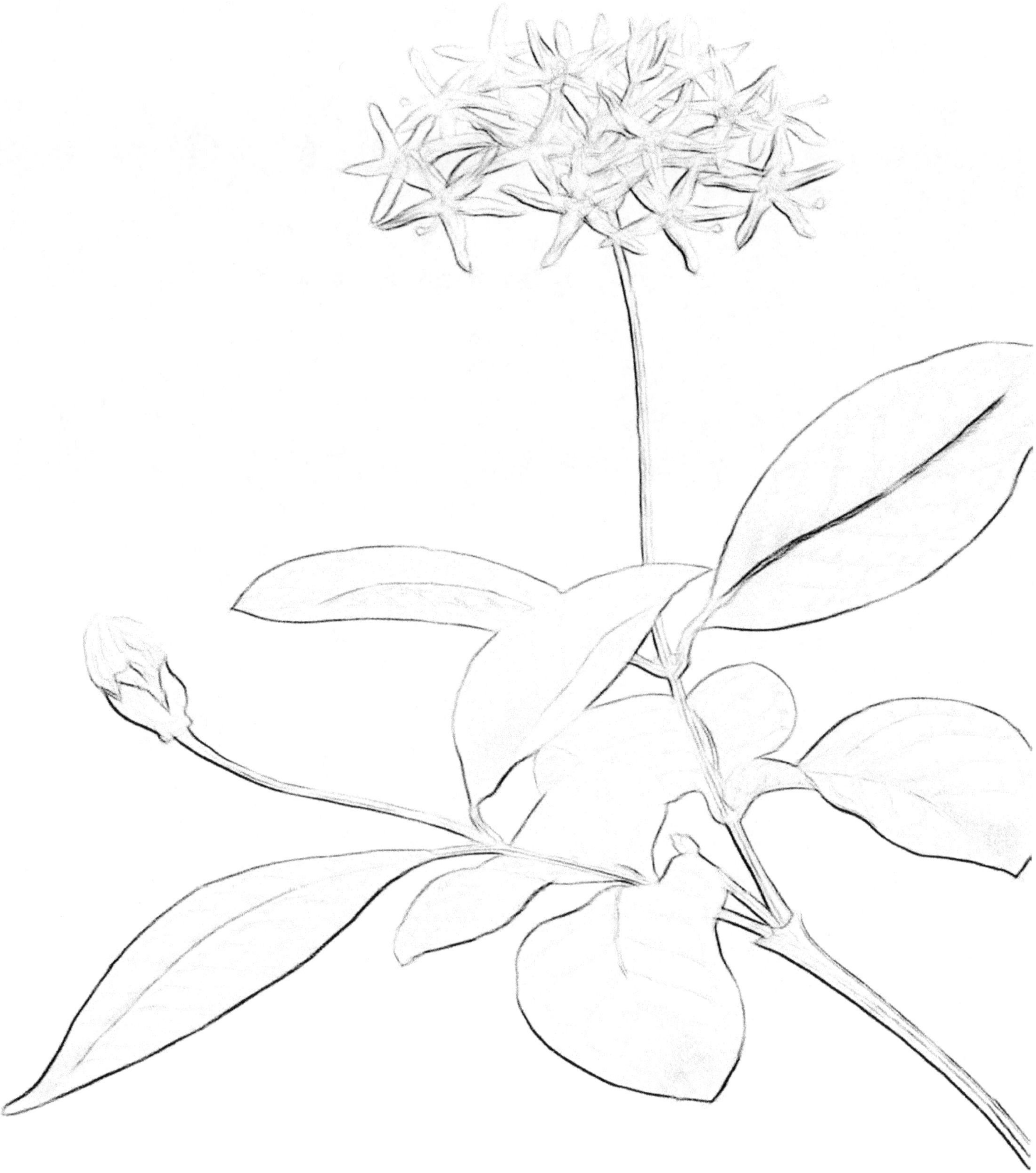

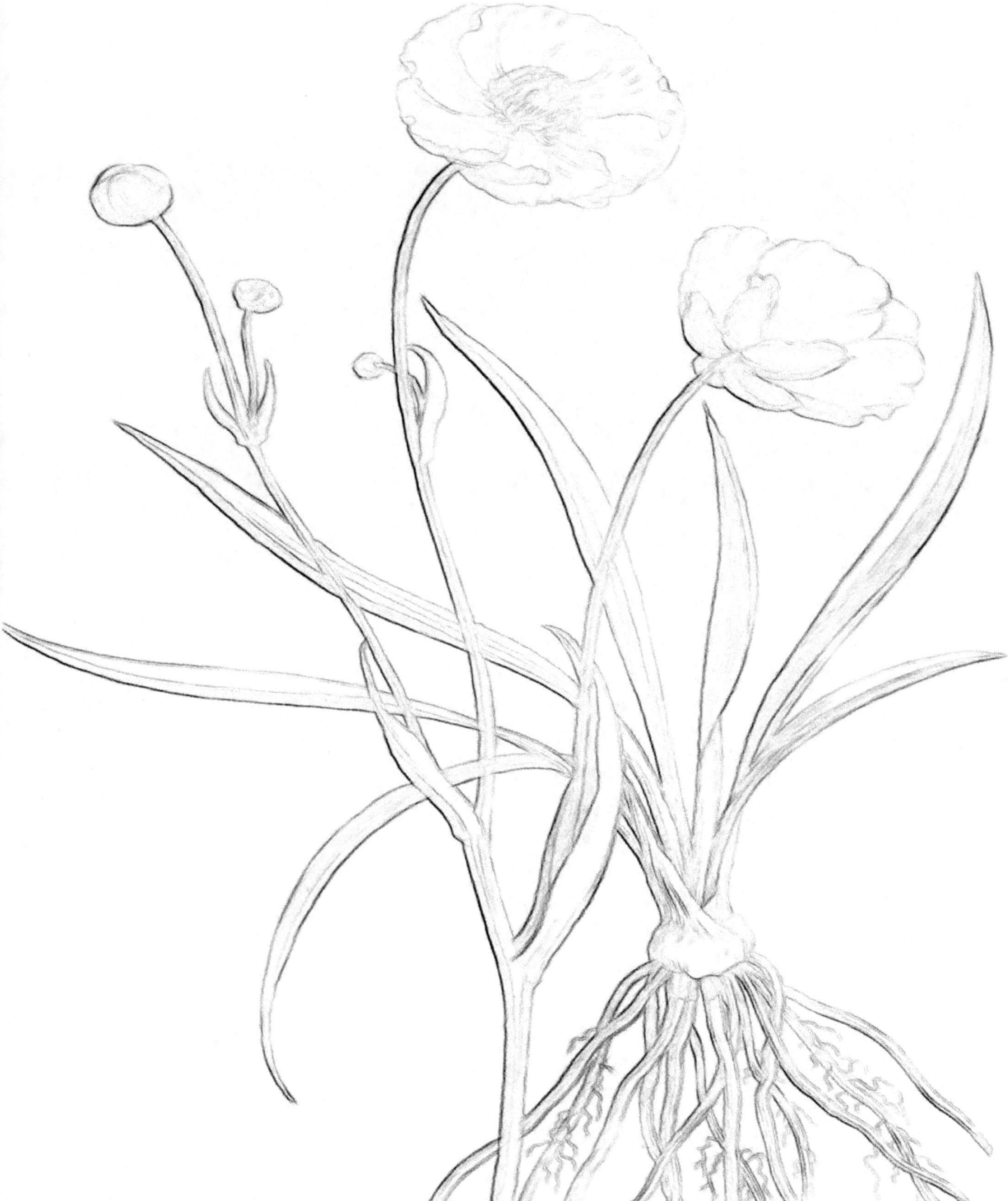

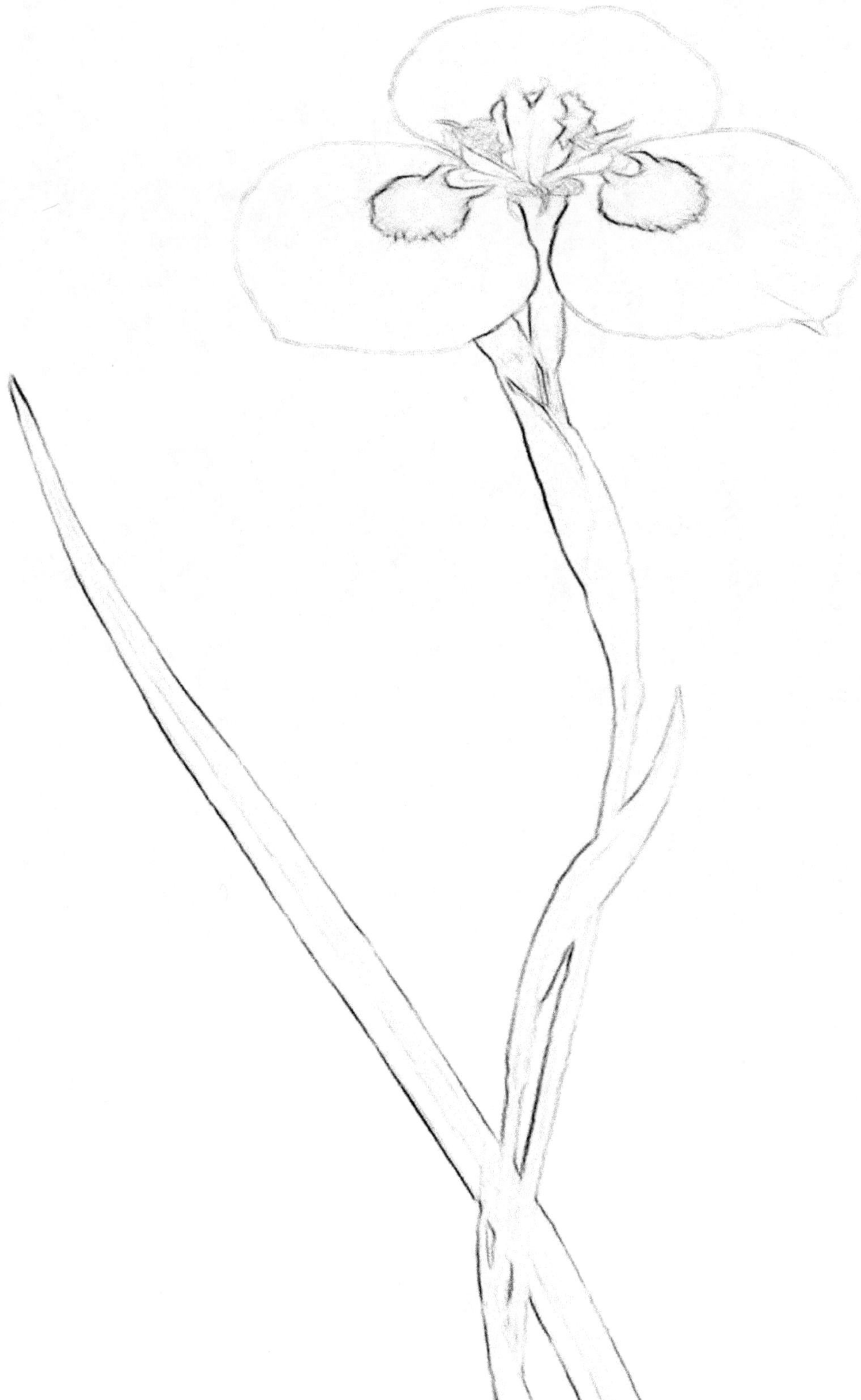

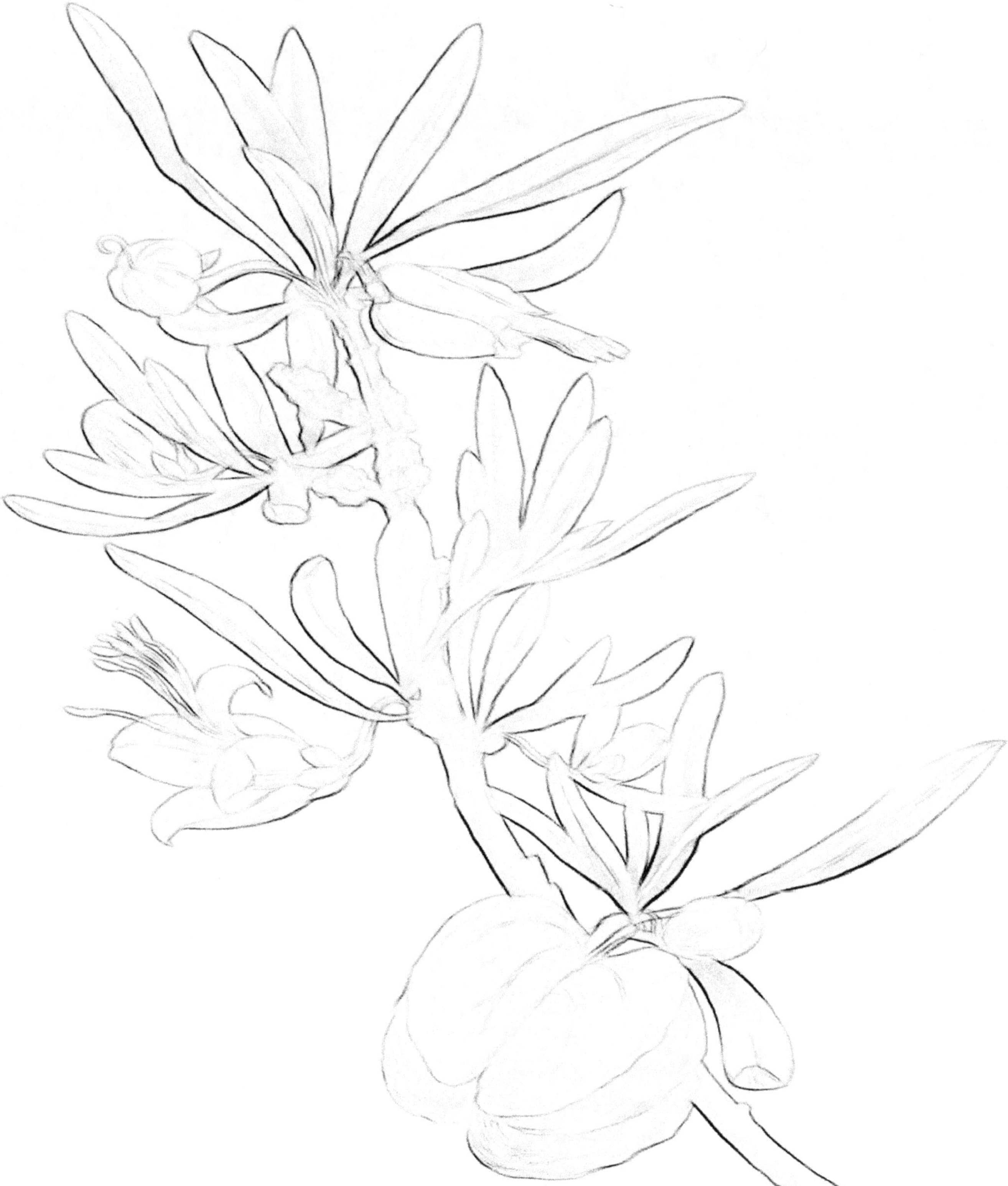

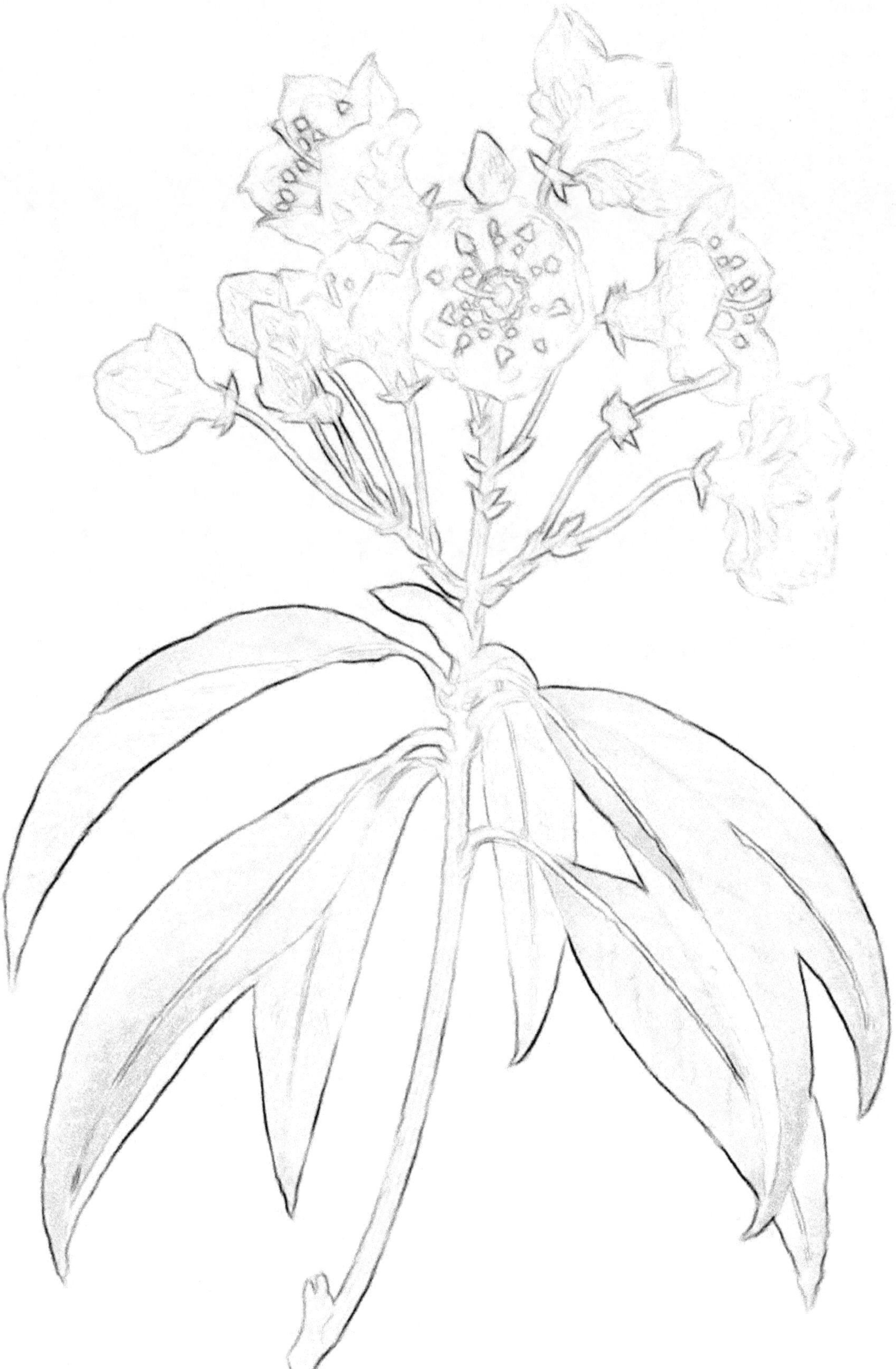

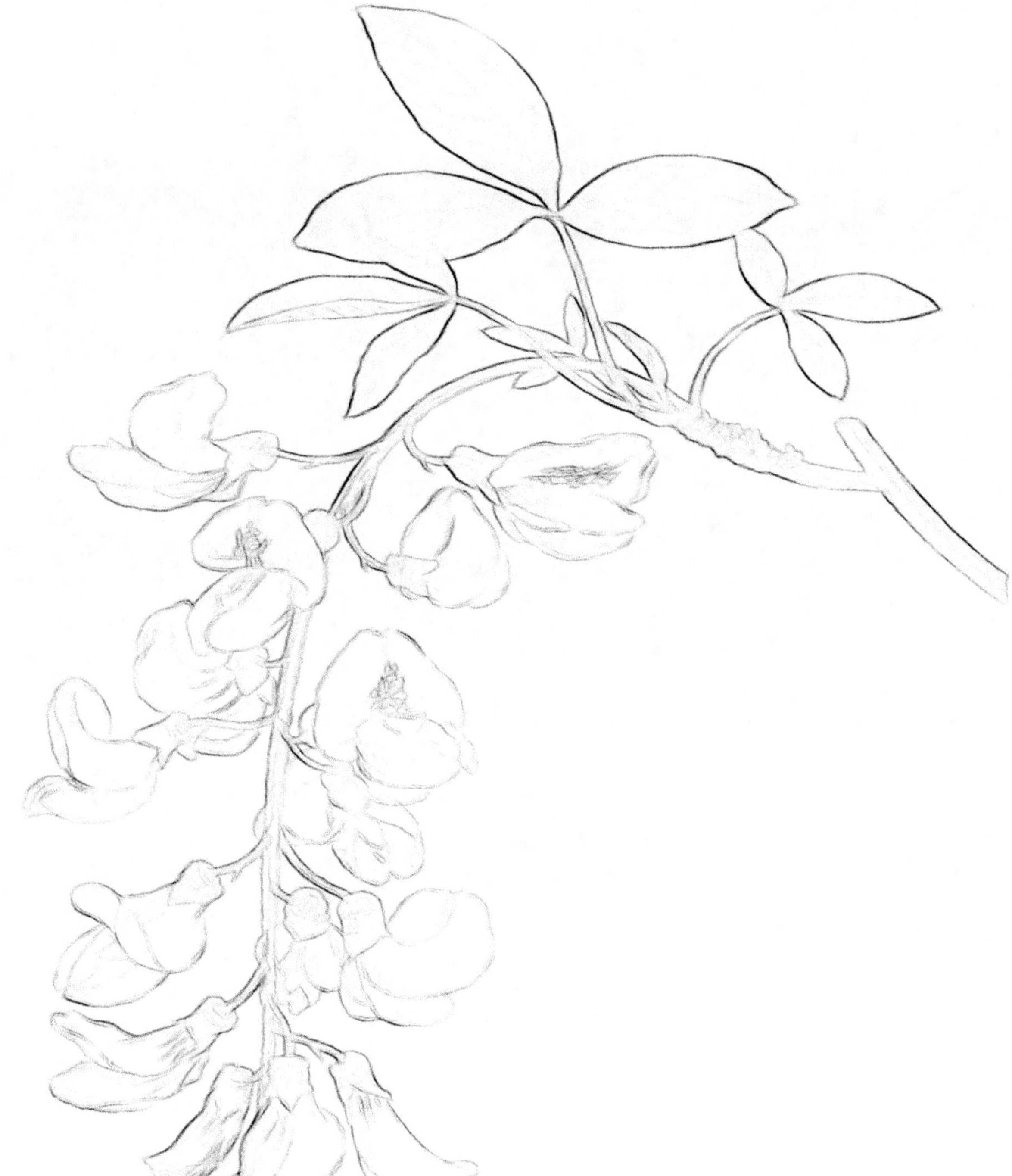

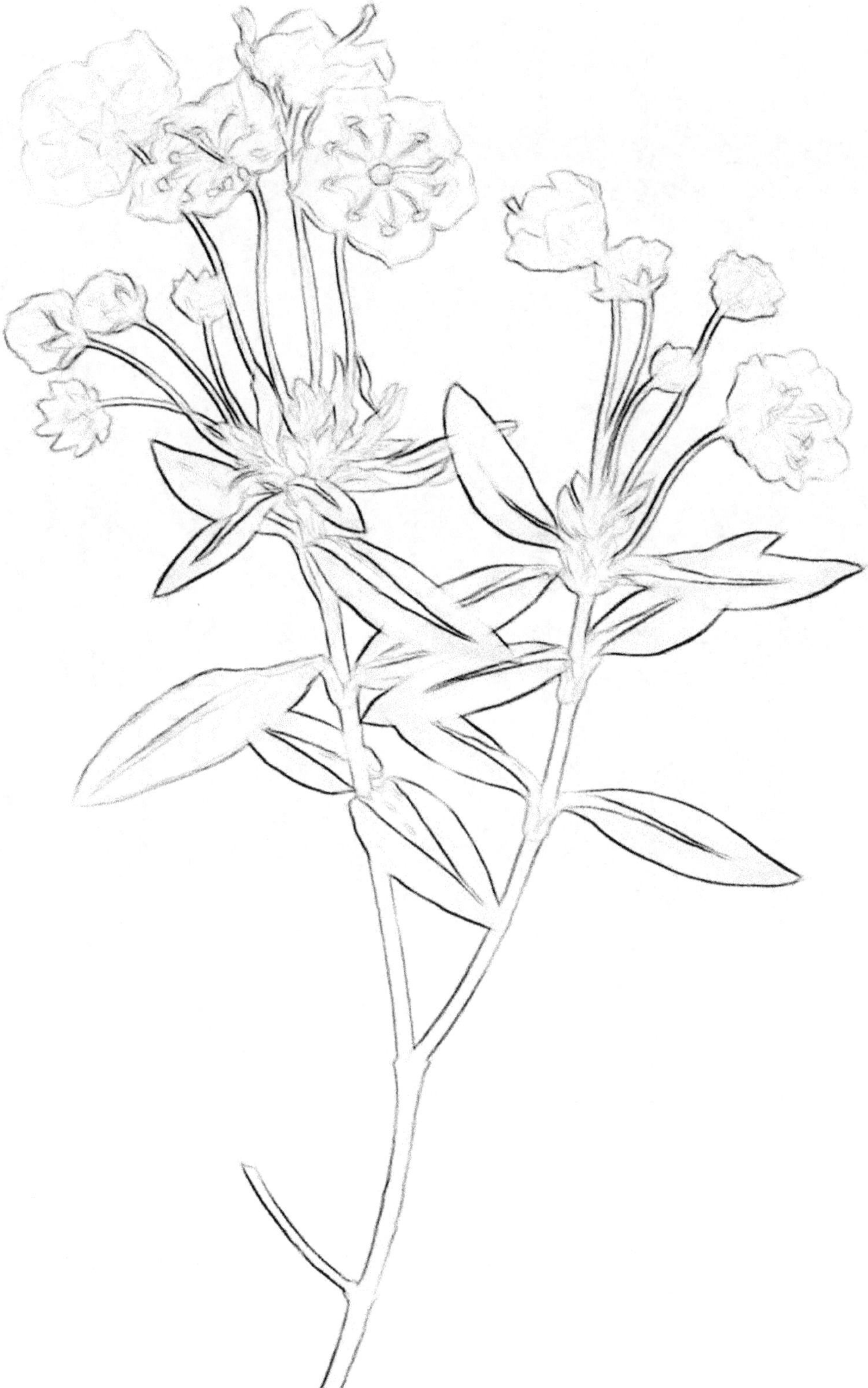

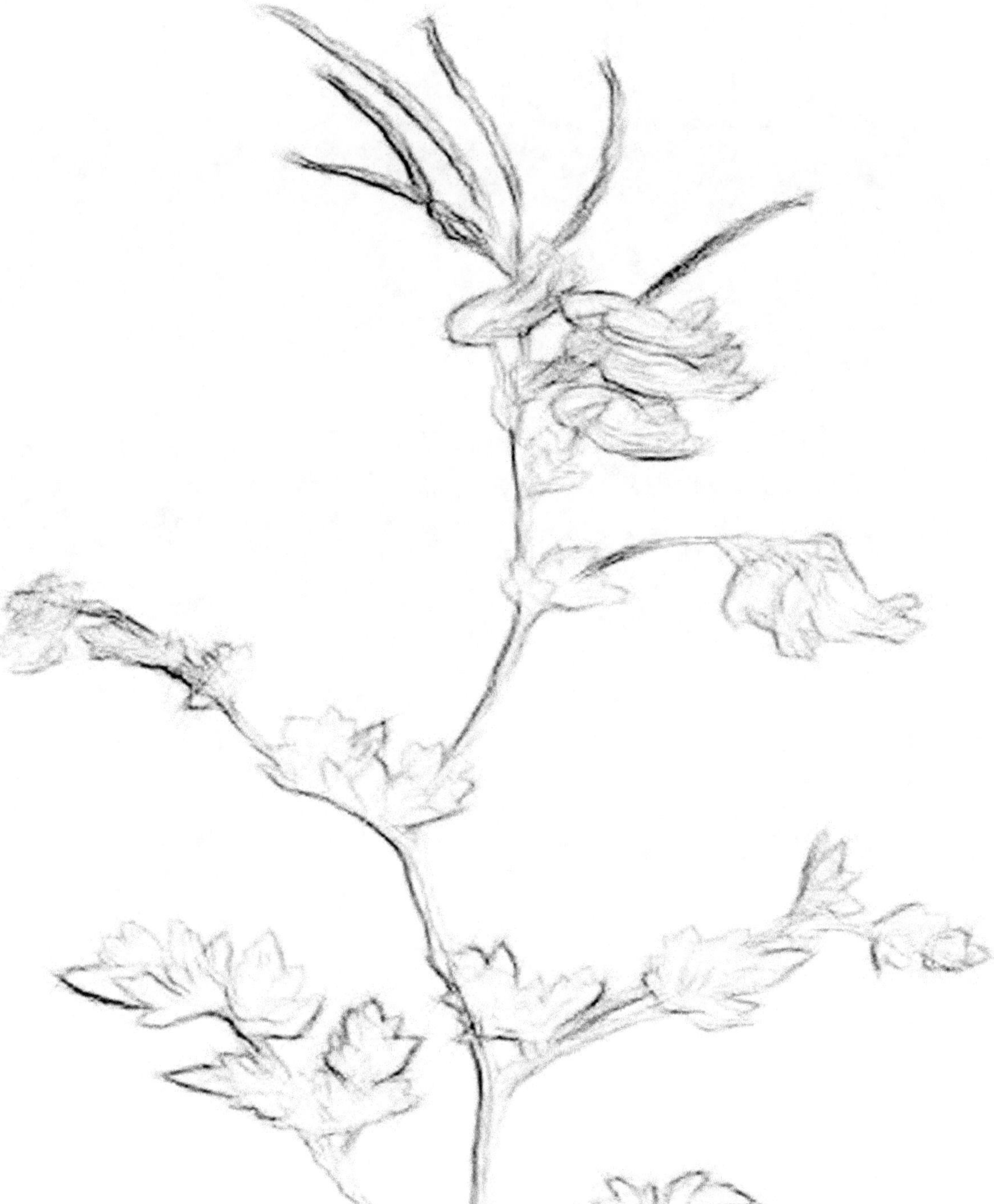

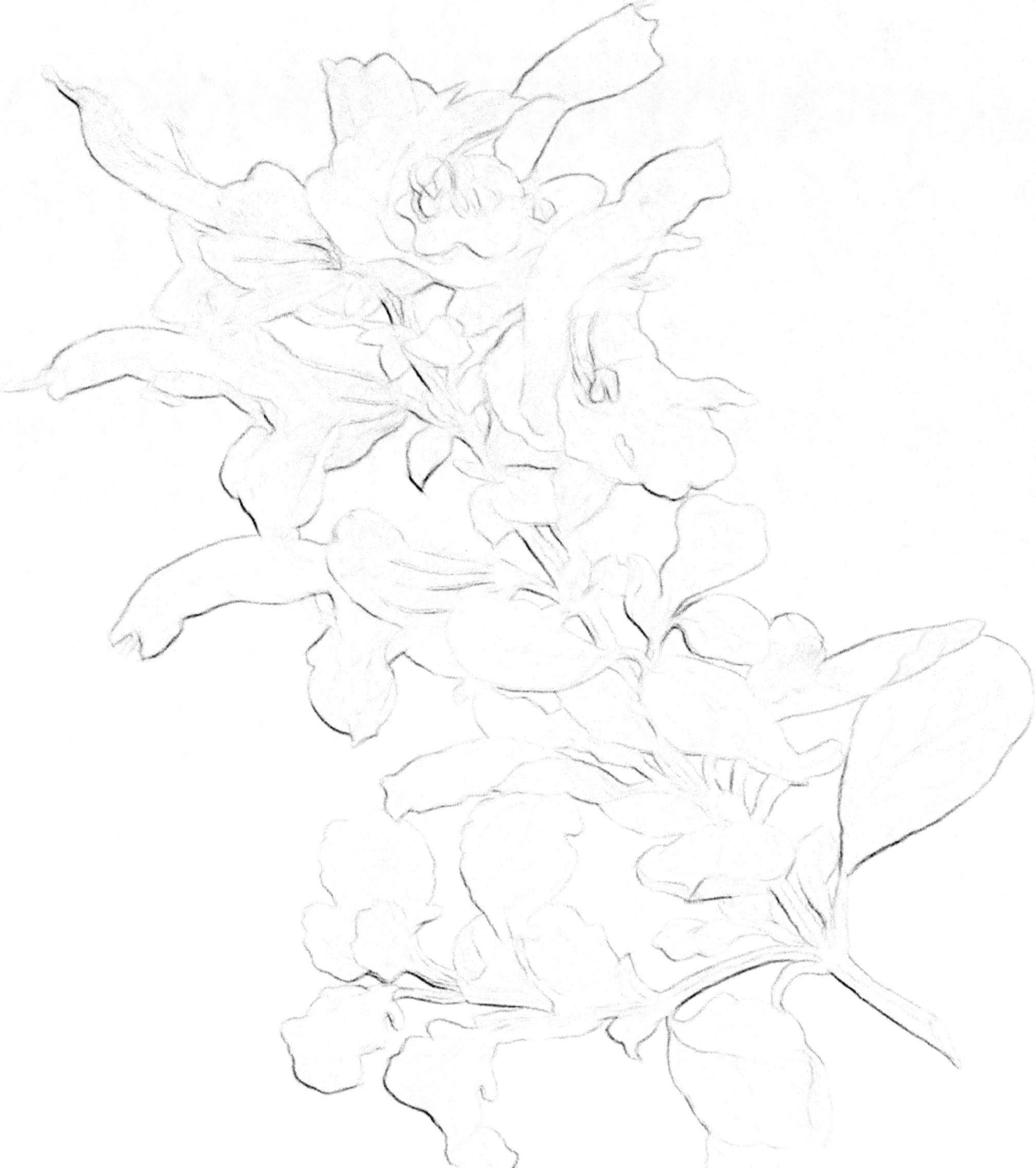

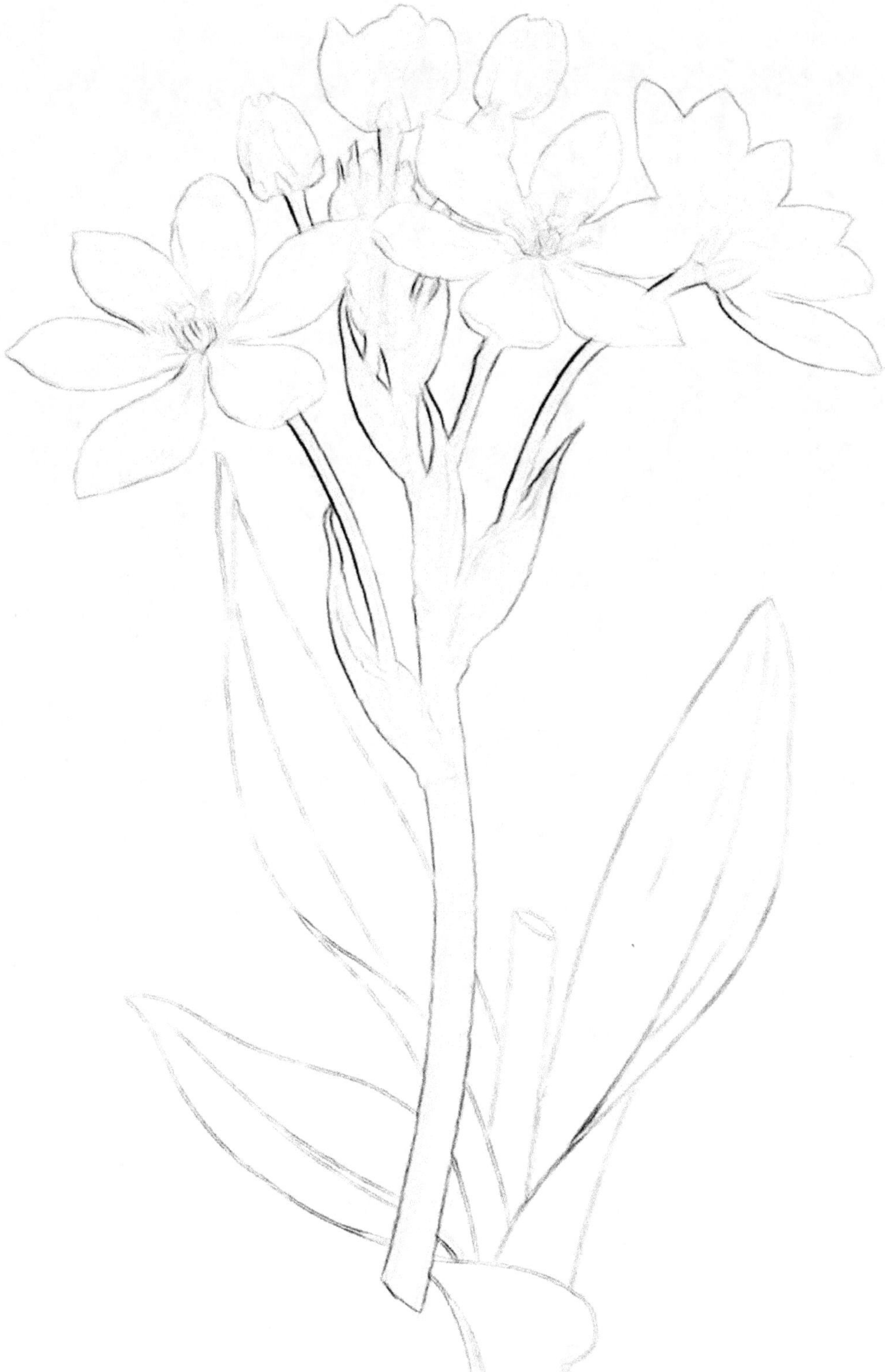

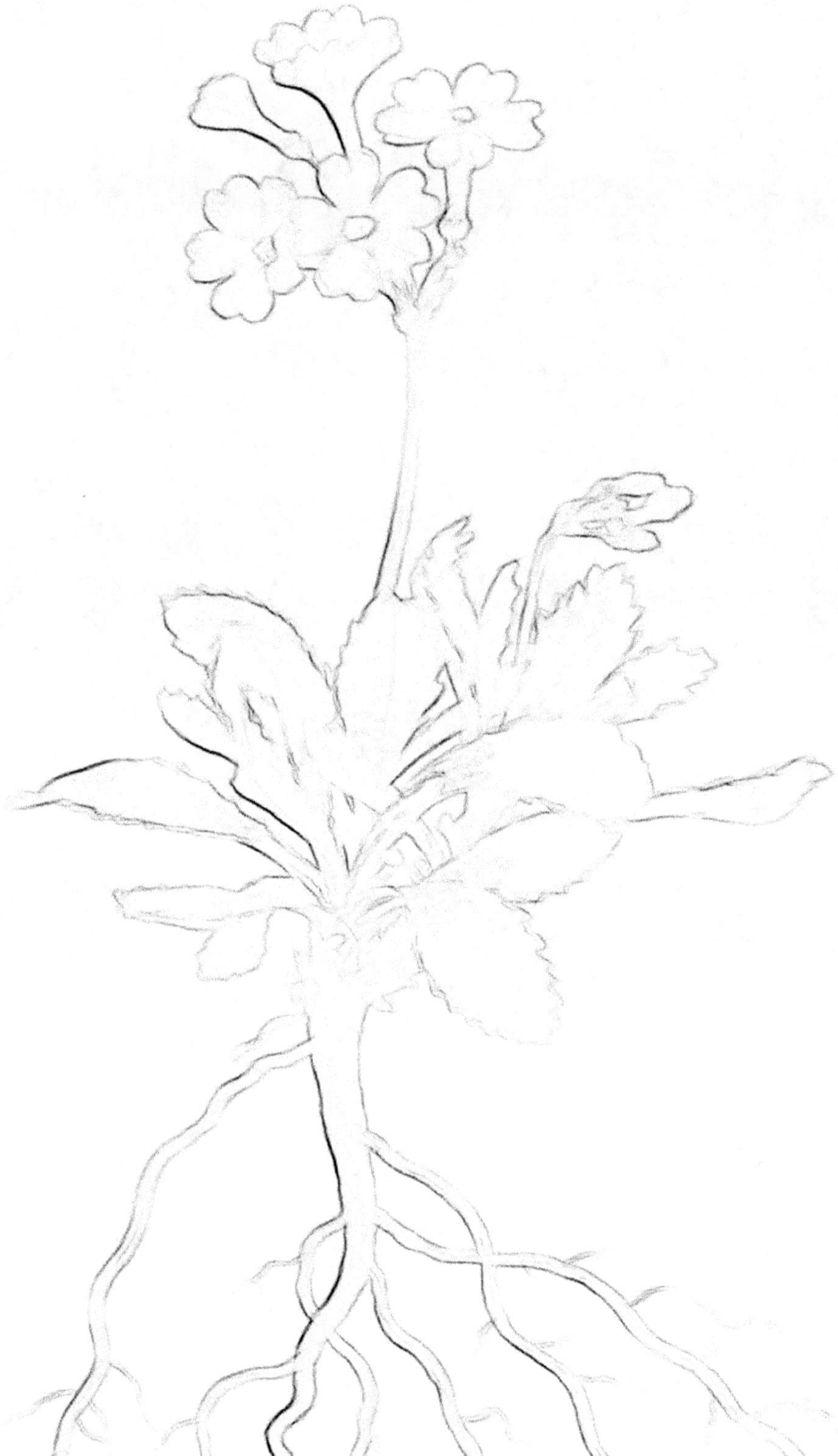

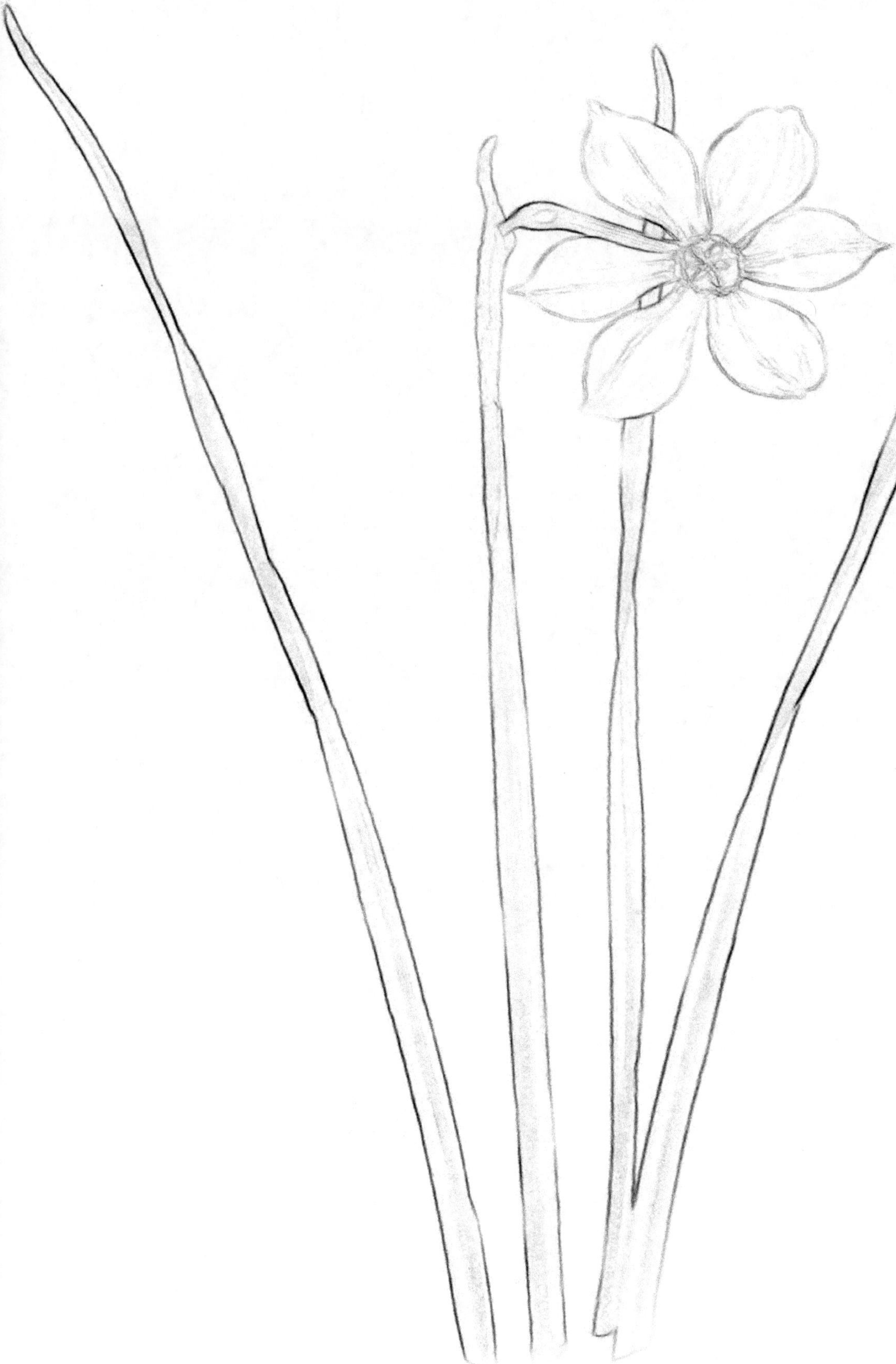

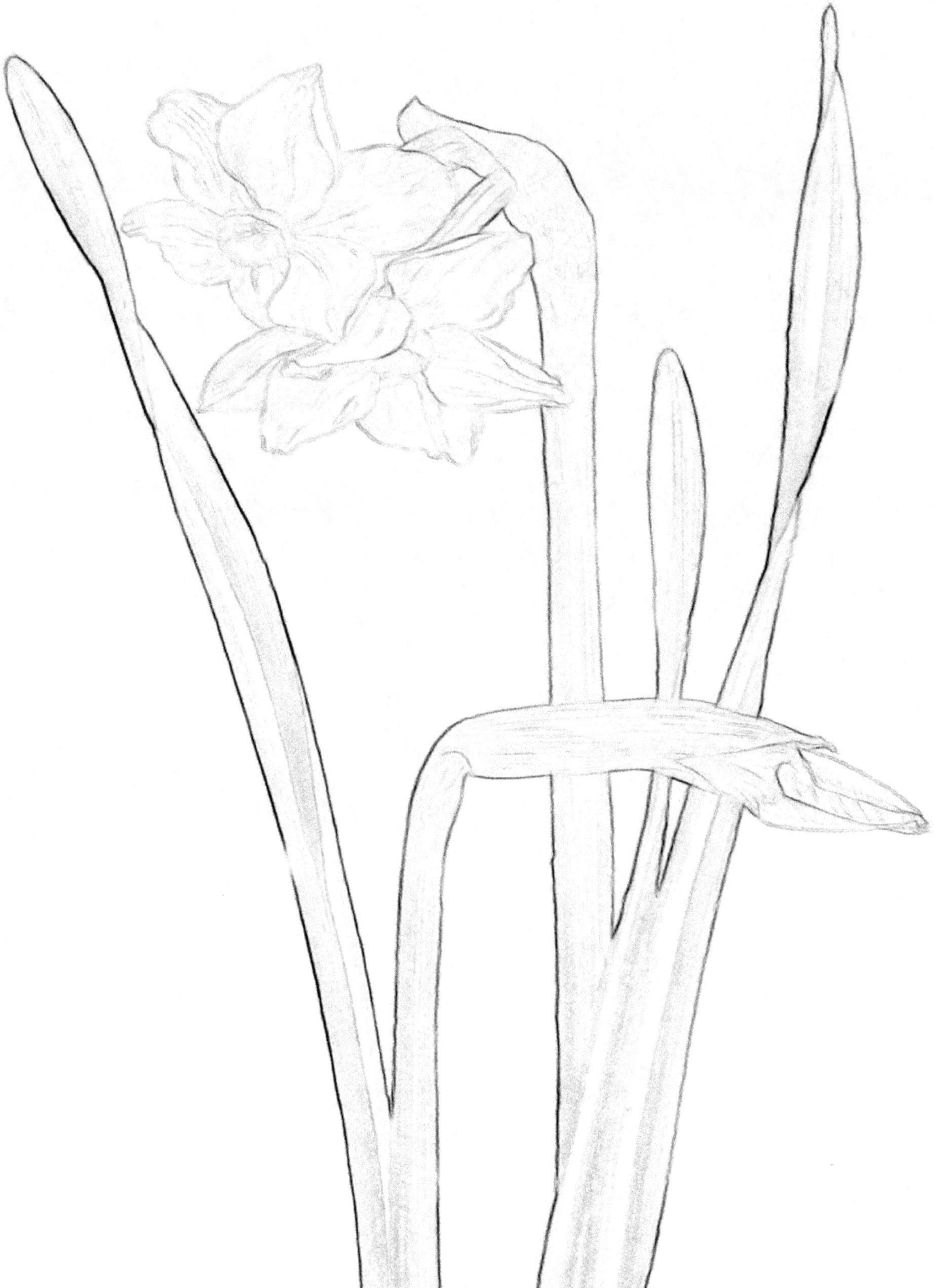

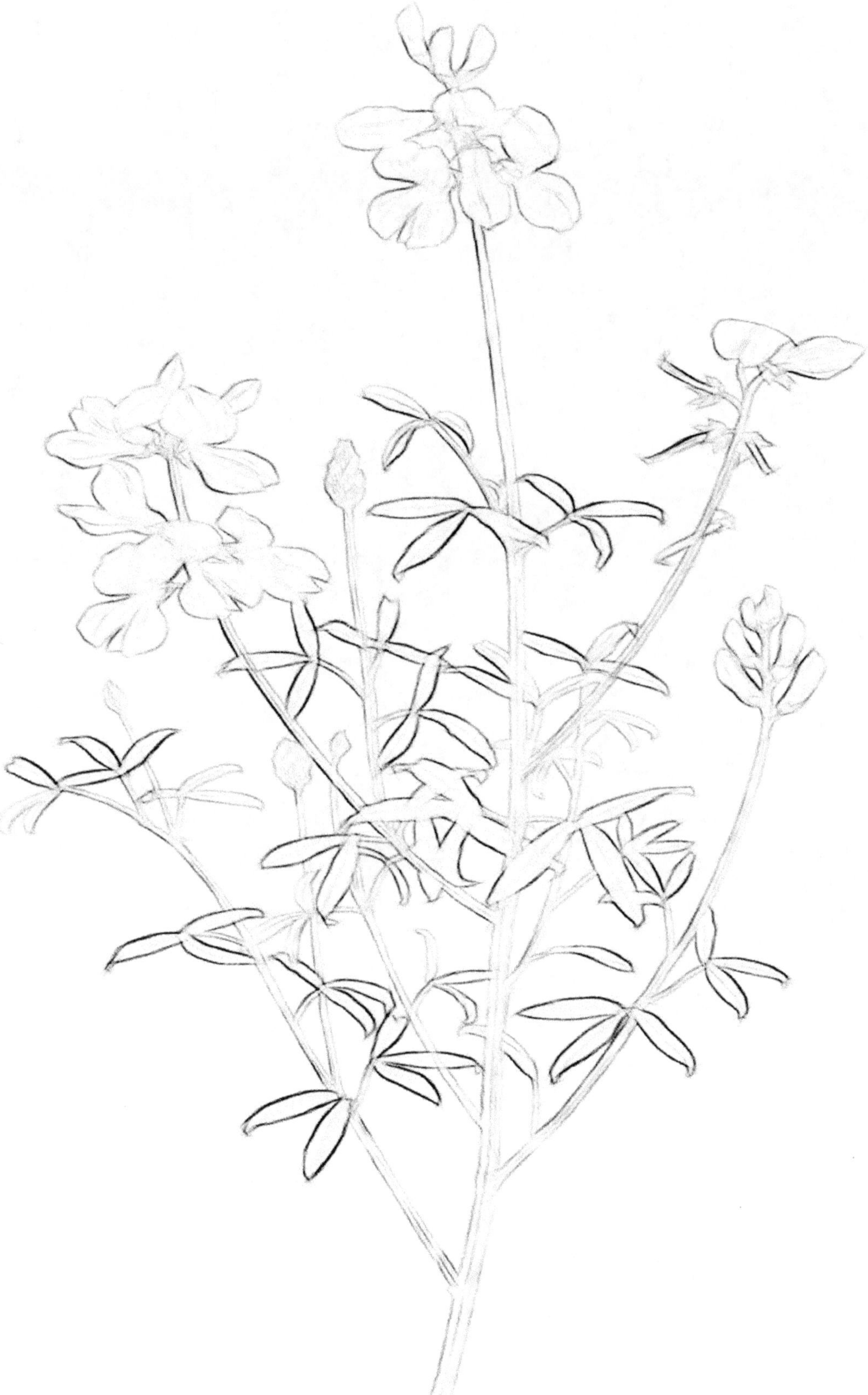

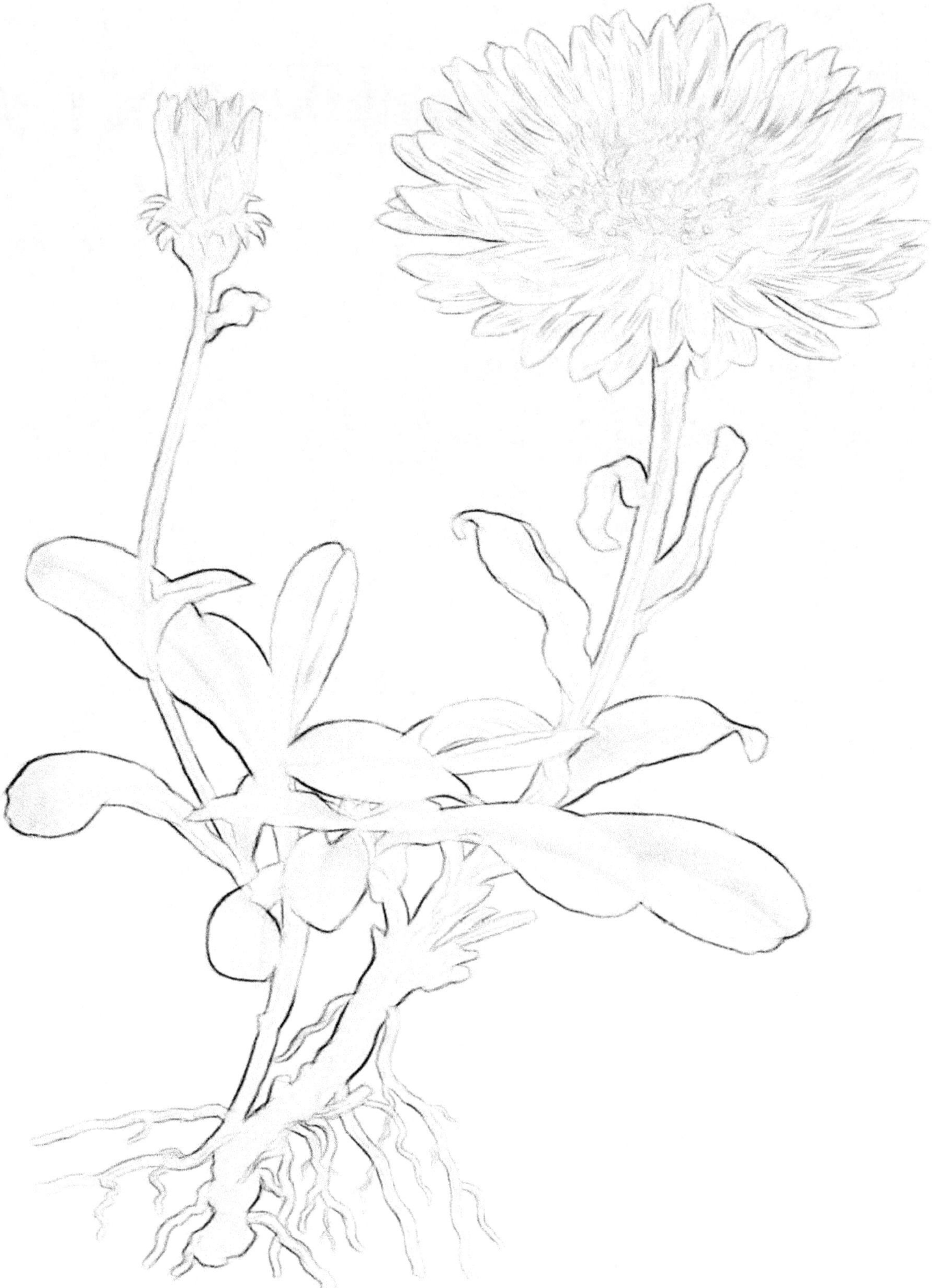

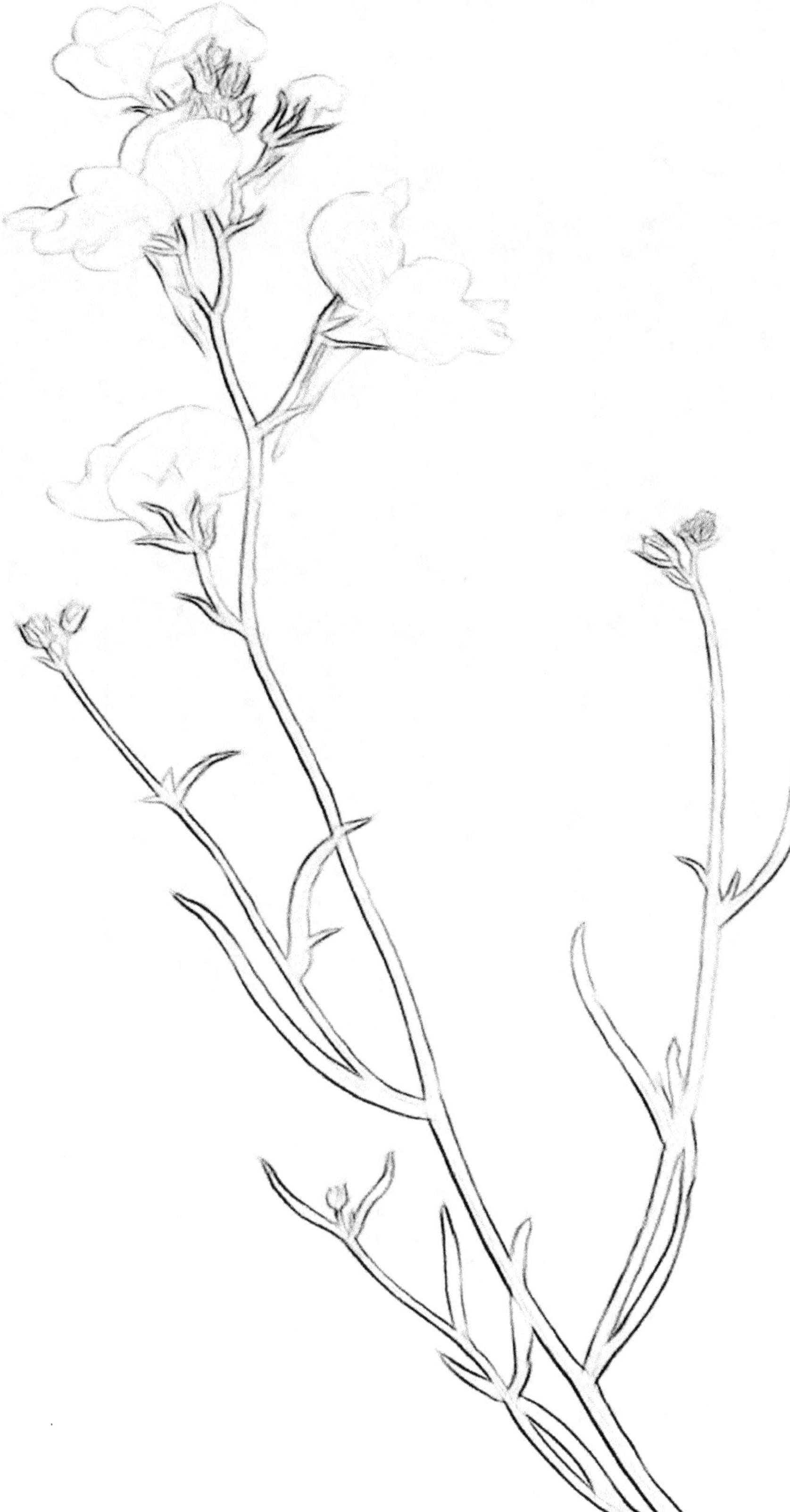

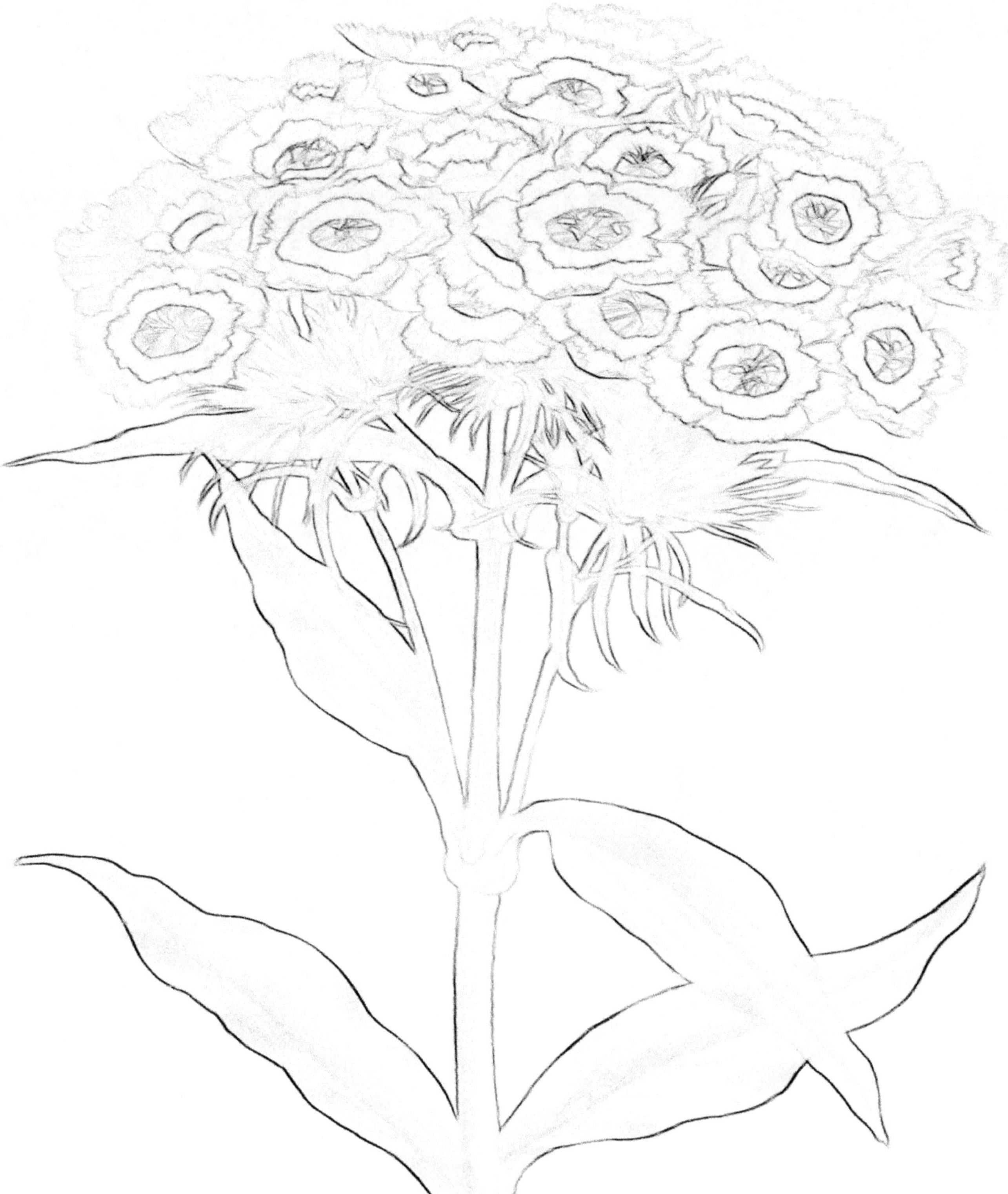

www.ingramcontent.com/pod-product-compliance
Lightning Source LLC
Chambersburg PA
CBHW080613180526
45168CB00007B/2893
* 9 7 8 1 5 1 5 3 0 1 0 6 6 *